How Animals Survive in the Cold

WRITTEN BY
Kelly Graham

It gets very cold in the Arctic!
Have you ever wondered how the
animals that live there survive
in the cold?

Different Arctic animals have different, special features and behaviours that help them live in the cold. These are called "adaptations."

This is a lemming. Lemmings usually stay under the snow in the winter. It is warmer under the snow.

Lemmings build nests out of grass, feathers, and fur. When lemmings sleep, they curl up together to stay warm.

Lemmings dig tunnels through the snow. They use their claws to dig up food like seeds, young plants, and the roots of plants.

Some types of lemmings have fur that turns white in the winter. This helps them blend in with the snow and hide from predators.

This is a muskox. Muskoxen have two layers of hair to help them stay warm.

They have long, shaggy hair that
protects them from the wind.
Underneath the shaggy hair, they have
a layer of soft hair called "qiviut."

Muskoxen have sharp hooves.
They use their hooves to dig through
hard-packed snow to get to the
plants below.

When there is a storm, muskoxen stand in a circle together. This lets them share the heat from their bodies.

This is an Arctic fox. Arctic foxes have very thick fur.

In the fall, Arctic foxes' fur changes colour to blend in with the snow and ice. It stays this way all winter. This helps them hide from predators.

Foxes have a strong sense of smell and hearing. This helps them find lemmings under the snow.

Foxes bury extra food in the snow to keep it fresh and to hide it from other animals. They return to their buried food when they are hungry.

This is a polar bear. Polar bears hunt on land and ice and in water.

Polar bears have thick fur. Under their fur, they have a layer of fat. Their fur and fat protect them from the cold wind and water.

In high winds, polar bears sometimes hide behind ice packs and ridges to stay warm.

Mother polar bears dig dens in the snow. They keep their young cubs in the dens, where it is warm and safe.

This is a ringed seal. Ringed seals spend a lot of time swimming through freezing-cold water.

Seals have a thick layer of fat called "blubber" under their skin to keep them warm.

Seals use their thick claws to make breathing holes in the ice. They scratch at the ice from underneath to keep their breathing holes open.

Human hunters and polar bears can wait patiently at breathing holes to catch seals.

This is a raven. Ravens have layers of small, soft feathers called "down" under their top feathers. This helps them stay warm.

Ravens build their nests on cliff ledges. The cliffs give them shelter from the wind. Their black feathers help them get heat from the sun.

Ravens eat parts of dead animals that bears, wolves, and humans leave behind.

In the winter, ravens spend more time near human communities. This is because it is easy to find food scraps left by people and dogs.

This is a snowy owl. Snowy owls are covered in warm feathers, even on their legs and toes.

They even have feathers that cover the sides of their beaks!

Snowy owls have a strong sense of hearing. They can listen for prey moving around under the snow.

They fly low over the ground and use their large talons to snatch up their prey.

There are a lot of animals that live in the Arctic. Animals need to have special adaptations to survive in the cold Arctic winters.